Pathways

and other poems

Poornima Dayal

BookLeaf Publishing

India | USA | UK

Made with ❤ on the BookLeaf Publishing Platform
www.bookleafpub.in
www.bookleafpub.com

Dedication

I dedicate this book to the Almighty Lord and thank Him
for guiding me through this journey.

Preface

This book is a compilation of 21 poems. These poems are on varied themes, some are highly imaginative and lucid in content. They also reflect my feelings and learnings from life. The narration is almost rhythmic in nature.

Poetry is almost as vast as the sea, exploring various emotions and situations in a poets life. This book is a combination of both fictional and non fictional poems. These poems also include the use of visual imagery and some of them have a slight romantic undertone to them.

Note- All the pronouns or archaic words starting with capital letters, usually refer to God.

Acknowledgements

I am grateful to God. I also thank my son, my husband, my mother and my dearest pet for always being so supportive in my artistic and poetic journey.

1. The Gulmohar tree

The Gulmohar tree swirling and dancing
to the rhythmic winds appeared to be singing,
and the leaves twirled, its flowers budding.
The mellow touch, from the winds above
filling their hearts with some unknown love,
a sight to watch from my open balcony
as I sit, relishing my spoonful of organic honey.

It's woody branches almost reaching the skies,
as within their homes my neighbour fried
some delectable sweets and savouries,
with some English tea, rich in flavory.
Like a canopy, sheltering small plants and bushes
when in such heat the gardener rushes
watering the tree and plants,
while aunt Ira loudly prays and chants.

The whispers of time, gathering no dust
as in the gardener, the tree fully trusts.
Its bright orange hue

under drops of fresh morning dew,
and when it rains, the petals glisten
almost asking us to stop and listen
to stories, tales of lovers perhaps,
resting under its shade is a burly, old chap.

It appears to be beaming and rejoicing,
almost as though it's love is approaching,
those Orange turning a passionate Red,
casting below a romantic, cosy bed.
Done to ashes are old, rustic leaves,
to those wooden branches, new petals cleave.

Bringing joys to my heart
regularly almost, as the day starts.
Cars passing by, some children running
to catch their school bus, every early morning.
Separating us, a distance of about
twenty feet,
the day begins and my neighbors do I almost daily greet.

The Suns rays harmonizing, bringing it light
as night falls, it rests, sleeping with great delight.
In peak summers, its time to blossom
and as they bloom, its just so awesome.
No deceit and no foul play
unfolding love, every night and day.

2. Light beyond the horizon

The misty shores,
like never before
the boat appears intact,
thats absolutely a fact.

Beyond the horizon, there is light
and though it may be at present out of sight,
desires are still plenty,
and things to do aplenty,
lets not burn them down,
nor in grief, must we drown.

Nothings ever permanent,
let the mists clear, leaving not even a remnant.
There is much hope,
and to achieve there is still scope.

Patience, they call it a virtue
theres no need for an internal curfew,

just wait but co create,
do all that it takes to recreate.

4

3. The Lord's leela (God's play)

Its so beautiful to stand under this shade,
of some divine wonder, it is made
under the Suns intense rays,
It sways.
A row of many,
sheltering so many,
a clear glimpse into the temple ahead,
for those standing below, and to the Lord, they may be
lead.

Near the stone and brick painted ground,
where so many flowers and pruned, small shrubs
surround.
Watching from somewhat a distance,
as people in queues wait with persistence.
Worshiping the deity, being their only motive,
the leaves playing to the winds, being emotive.

In the subtle whispers of the day,

under those loud and radiant rays,
where measures of time could be given a pass,
and near the roots are growing shiny blades of grass.

Krishna's Idol central to a blue pond,
fish swimming and dancing, its like a lovers bond.
His flute, a golden blue
their skin a blackish hue,
floating and swimming near His feet,
their hearts for their Lord, lovingly beat.

Sounds of loud bells tolling,
chants of ' Hare Krishna', so alluring,
albeit, from a distance may be heard,
before him all else, stands absolutely blurred.

They continue moving - oh these trees are grooving,
to sounds of 'Mridangams', Sparrows appear to be
crooning,
a part of such chorus, where the Lord is being praised,
as children are thronging , the curtains being raised.

Hare Krishna Hare Krishna
Krishna Krishna Hare Hare
Hare Rama Hare Rama
Rama Rama Hare Hare.

4. This is love

I love you ,
Do I ?.
My heart's not a broken wing,
feelings so new, life does bring.
Its fluttered, its flapped
its enjoyed, its clapped,
in short moments of despair, it may have even clamped,
not one man's name has it eternally stamped.

Seasons of spring
wearing a heart-shaped ring,
seasons of winters,
the fire place shinning like bliinters,
in summers when the light shone bright,
did emerge a well dressed knight.
And what about Autumn,
was love, scraping the bottom?.

No, love is eternal,
from some lover or felt as paternal,

holding my hands, I wish he would dance
forever and ever, not missing any chance.
Is there a longing,
or a desire for belonging,
perhaps not, cause I know
am happy just being in the flow.

There may have been many,
but for such I cant move a penny,
not that they lacked
or whilst pursuing they slacked,
it just didn't click,
not even as some kind of flick.

This love is so precious, hold onto to it tight
within our very being is it's gorgeously glowing light.
Let no one plunder,
don't ever make that blunder
even if you do fall in love with a man,
don't allow that heat to burn or tann.

To feel love is a must,
not allowing ourselves to melt in lust,
is important to feel good
all so called calamities, has this notion withstood.

Bowing to the grace of love,

it's wonders blessing us from above,
embracing its every part with gratitude,
theres always that infinite latitude.

5. Fascinating life

The glittering skies under the Moon,
with fluttering leaves, in the month of June.
A note so sweet may be heard,
somewhere in the world, strolls an Elephant's herd.

The luminous night is shinning through,
bringing joys and love to more than a few.
Passive waters in the sea,
whispering songs like a honey bee.

Evening now becomes a shadow,
slipping into the night , as it follows.
And time has flown by from youth,
waves caressing the trodden sands, as they soothe.

Battling ties and relationships,
building bonds and new friendships.
The Moon shone bright above the soft, wet sands,
forming some sort of silvery, glowing bands.
Rain drops resting above those shapely clouds,

Singing nightingles, they do us proud.

Hark, a moment please,
somewhere, some one may be wanting a release.
A lightening storm may be brewing,
in the dark of the night, the Gods may be reviewing.

Redeeming themselves from such a past,
where reflections of that night may have cast.
Sullied by the grime of bygone age
making way out of a so called cage.

The dimming stars fade away...
giving birth, every night and day.

The Sun is rising above the mist,
in every tale, theres an interesting twist.
Like molten love, melting the snow
a rosy, light future, where new borns grow.

6. Holy Mother

Wearing Her gorgeous blue cloak,
She is revered by many a folk.
In her arms she lovingly holds
Her baby Jesus, and all Her love unfolds.

His eyes so magnanimous
watching, blessing a life so harmonious,
That halo above their heads so divine,
drizzlring rays of hope upon us so sublime.
If only I could be present
or perhaps may be I was a peasant,
in days of yore,
when needed not man alot more,
when they walked the Earth,
making life well worth.
I would serve Thee
without any fee.
I would wash Thy feet
and my eyes, so blessed as they would meet,
Thy feet so pure

that my heart would be cured.
Still, hold my hands
so I may land ,
in every life
living, without any strive.
Give me the joys of washing my sins
with Thy holy waters, that Ye may bring,
drinking and bathing in the Lourdes,
would be a gift from my beloved Lord.
Oh, nights I'd spent plenty, in pressing Thy hands
as Ye my Mother, so wonderfully do stand.
Offering a Rose or two,
or may be more than just a few,
garlanding Thee with boundless love,
as Ye may be blessing me from above.

That sprinkling, holy water, in churches sometimes with
added Rock salt,
healing my heart, forgiving all my faults.
The gifts Ye offer, oh my sweet Goddess,
purifying my thoughts that may have been of less.

Your bosoms, holding close my Lord,
for us is like an eternal reward.
Sacred heart of my supreme mother,
Sacred heart, of my revered father,
give me virtues, so Ye I may please

any upsetting thoughts, in me may cease.
Give me Joy and love so good,
teach me with Thy sermons, more than I may have
understood
in ways so loving and soothing my mind,
oh, my parents, Though art so kind.

Wearing Her gorgeous blue cloak,
She is revered by many a folk...

7. The Fakir

The tiny, old fakir,
walking away from the Gir,
in hot summers months,
running away from all fronts.
Of life was he tired,
and differently was he wired,
moving away from so called battles,
moving slowly with a herd of cattle,
of animals he was fond,
with them he had a close bond.
His cheeks had sunk in,
with hair, that were black and thin,
his skin, almost dark and tanned,
as he had travelled across many a sea and lands.

Living a life of dogma and rules,
traveling also with his wonderful friend, a mule.
He carried with him this old bag,
stitched together were some torn and tattered rags.
Across many forests and jungles he travelled,

breathing in new, fresh air as he marvelled,
at lifes self nurturing ways,
walking bare feet , almost every day.

His tiresome ways of life giving way to new born
excitement,
beginning to meditate, under a tree shade with
enticement
hoping that one day he would get enlightened,
choosing a path of reverence, for him was heightened.
Closing his eyes, he began
he was a truly disciplined man.

And the skies cast afresh
the blues and yellows, covering him like a mesh.
Many a crows and Mynas wondering around
watching him soundly hold his ground,
once or twice a hornbill appeared
the fakir by now had grown a long, white beard.

His skin a woody brown,
as the lights shown above his crown,
reflecting shimmery beams of moon light
his face glowing bright,
in those stellar nights.

Turning into a mahatama or a guru,

of his identity, the passers by had no clue.
A fakir once, but now a swami?,
certainly far away was he from those living a life quite
palmy.

A fragment of my imagination,
a vision, is it out of some citation,
weaving together, threads of old, simplistic stories,
devoid are they of mathematics or theories.

8. Welcoming love

The heart skips a beat,
is this love, again a repeat
when he loved me so
or I felt it at every go,
when he sang a song
and it didn't take me that long
to embrace and hug,
feeling my heart tug,
holding his fingers
while he lingered
in my garden filled with plentiful roses,
as we swirled and danced in various poses.

This time, this love may be different,
I have grown, but I cant be indifferent.
Glaring at my eyes, as he does,
I move towards him without any fuss.
Oh, this love, I say
why must you happen again in the month of May,
now stay on forever, today and everyday.

Is love trying to happen again,
and am I now going to regain,
pleasures of such romantic love,
like that of gentle romantic doves,
the reawakening of that wild fire,
flaming embers of passionate desire.
Lets keep this love a secret this time,
these nights are precious, just your's and mine.

Our love will blossom more in June,
lets dance to all the melody and tune.
Oh, its not fake
and lets no longer make
excuses or hide all feelings so pure,
and me your warmth does definitely lure.

Oh my beloved, look at the stars,
as you have come from a distance so far,
In the morning when the Sun will rise,
wrapped in a cosy blanket, as we will arise,
our love getting brighter, will be more wise.

Thank Ye Lord, for showering it upon me,
theres so much more to look forward and see.
The waves glittering like shimmery pearls,
as this delightful, new season of love unfurls.

Age doesn't hinder
its infact a binder,
in your case and mine,
oh, such gifts from the divine.

Fare you well,
my darling,
in love, my heart doth swell
and even when we are miles apart,
or till our bodies depart,
let us enjoy and play our part,
listening gleefully to the voice of our hearts.

9. Let me not barge in

And the world may crumble,
I think they shouldn't rumble.
Though science is great where discoveries are made,
however going beyond the head and mind may not
actually be laid.
You may make the finest planes or copters,
travel to the moon and back in a chopper,
you may be an astronaut, walking galaxies,
or deriving pleasure out of building fantasies,
but creating new life
through inception or a knife,
trying to remould organisms,
hence igniting your fancies and whims,
through artificial means
on which a scientist may lean,
is not so breezy,
and sounds very cheesy.

Human life isnt eternal in mind or body,
theres a limit till where it may craft a new toddy.

Don't try to insist that you can do
let somethings be, they may be many or few.

I just read a story about hatching a Dodo,
re-engineering a Nicobar pigeon, you should say no to.
Let them be and let them fly,
disturbing nature's bounties, they shouldn't even try.

Being a commoner, I may not be heard,
though a humble request in all these words,
let nature create its only rhapsody,
without interference from science or anybody.
Ofcourse, as a subject it must be taught,
so much to learn and gain from its lot,
the Divine will guide you,
for He is kind,
not taking advantage, is what this may remind.
Do not allow such moments to end this Earth,
enjoy and nurture, its every worth.

These are just my thoughts,
not much knowledge have I got,
Am just a little fish, swimming in this ocean so vast,
don't fight the system and end it so fast.

Don't crush mother Earth,
this shouldn't bring about false mirth,

she is for us to love,
such acts are only of unlove,
nourishing your ego,
or may be from heavens you have a go,
let me not barge in or speak my heart,
perhaps, its what the Lord dictates as you sincerely play
your part.

10. The Kirtan

A gathering of pilgrims assembled,
a glowing, sacred sage - the Kirthankar, resembled.
Combining various hyms and holy verses,
chanting from holy texts, such dedicated words and
phrases.

'Oh my beloved, Though art so pure,
Thy holy hands and magic are such a lure'................
'Since times immemorial,
since eternity, or may be beyond,
with warmth and love you surround....
my being , my very soul, within you
and with each birth and time ,Ye renew'............

' Your merciful touch, Your love - filled glances,
immersed in you, oh, my heart dances.
Leading me on is Thy spring of holy waters,
bathing and washing my sins from all quarters'..............

'Sparkling lights of love from above,

filling my heart, oh, with such ethereal love.
Though art in Heaven and on land,
Though art in water and in the sands.
Though art in air,
to the holy throne, the only heir,
Though art in space,
blessing me with Thy, holy grace'........

'As Ye fill my heart so tender,
of Thy presence, theres always a reminder.
May I caress those feet, so holy
oh, my Lord, upon seeing you ,I am jolly'..............

'Born to you - of you, Oh Mighty
nurtured and nourished by you, so rightly.
I know not what this world would mean,
had Ye not kept me in Thy sheen'.......

'My spoon is filled with Thy sweet nectar,
polishing me, you are my only lector.
Oh, my heart would swell if you would appear,
intimating beforehand, when you may be near.
In your lap, I will rest
it is my only cosy nest'..........

'Thou art my father and my mother,
Thou art my aunt and my brother ,
Though art my friend, my confidant
on Ye I rely, I cry and to you I rant.
Picking up my threads,
guarding them from becoming shreds,
I eat Thy loaf and vegetable mince,
hoping my heart and mind may be rinsed'............

'Take me oh, Ye Lord, onto Thy shores,
or am I already being sailed by Thy oars,
Pick me up - don't drop me down
let me see Thy majestic crown'.

And such hyms and verses, he belted,
while my heart and theirs melted.
What a harmonious day it is,
lets listen and glorify, lets not give it a miss.

11. Pathways

Doorways opening,
doorways closing.
Pathways meandering,
pathways leading.
Doorways guiding,
doorways brightening.
Windows glaring,
windows reflecting.
Sun's rays showering,
Sun's rays entering.
Windows glowing,
windows beaming.
Doorways widening,
doorways seeking.
Traveller's alighting,
traveller's passing.
Pathways swerving,
pathways narrowing,
Tress passers turning,
tress passers rushing.

Windows highlighting
windows concealing,
Sparrows resting,
sparrows sneaking.
Doorways calling,
doorways enthralling.
New borns crying,
new borns laughing,
Pathways screaming,
pathways winding.
Visitors contemplating,
visitors surviving.
Windows peaking,
windows sliding.
Granny's approaching,
grandpa's advancing.

12. Alhamdollilah

Today I spoke to an old friend,
reminding me of lovely Omani trends,
of greeting and blessing
love to their dear ones, are they always expressing.
His words so pure,
in my mind did cure,
bringing more respect
to that loving aspect
of their traditions and generosity
of which there isn't a paucity.

Wishing me good,
this nature of his has stood,
through months and years,
even though we haven't met, through all my lears.
God maketh men, few or perhaps many like him,
and I continue living, praying and reciting a hymn.
Thanking him today through these verses I Pray,
may he be blessed with more bounties his way,
may our children be happy,

our families be favoured,
may the Lord shower His adoration
upon His every creation.

Talking to him yesterday revived more hope,
believing in humanity, no, its not all a joke.
Somewhere exists still love, selfless and pure
about this I am now, oh, so sure.
Look up and we will find,
Look around and we will find,
Look beneath and we shall find
sparks of reality,
existing in all
there ain't a duality,
it may be day light or night fall.

Making an obeisance to the mighty Divine,
for bringing such moments in my life, so fine.

13. Art-a gift

Art cant be finite,
for me its scape is infinite,
a gift from the Almighty,
its not to be taken lightly.
Its just too magnanimous,
its vibes are harmonious,
within the light it blends,
as different colors to it the artist lends.

Every action is a piece of art,
performing it like a holistic craft,
it could even be a simplistic act,
of drawing just a line, and thats a fact.
Its what pours out from you or me,
for art lovers to comprehend or see,
why make it complicated,
unless the heart has such dictated.

Some say they cant even draw a line,
they should just leave it to the Divine,

let it reveal, there must be something else
ice freezing, upon heating does melt.

I am no artist and I know,
painting or writing doesn't make me so,
I just follow, walking on that path,
its a prized treasure that we hath.

14. The tailor

The dexterous tailor,
once recieved a mailer
to stich and sew,
some dresses anew.
With heavy hands and long, slim fingers,
with a heart of gold but quite a thinker.
Beginning to iron out the clothes till every grain,
holding the edges, avoiding any stain.
A crisp, bridal Orange, Tissue cloth
with tints of antique gold, resembling a tasty Chicken
broth.
Sticking floral sequins and motifs
to prepare the best was his only motive.
Grooming brides and grooms alike
draping them in outfits that they would like.
Spending hours at his sewing machine
under a fan was he daily sweating like a stream.
Yet, worrying not of the heat or cold,
he, at 60 was certainly very bold.

With eyes gaping through his old, rugged spectacles
making dresses as fancy spectacles,
quivering hands, yet, finding the right strand
to stitch and sew
there weren't many like him, not even a few.
A burgundy coat, once he did stitch
belonging to the nobles, oh they were just so rich.
Handing him coins of Silver, did they award
for his amazing craft, he recieved a reward.

Toiling under a thin, metal sheet
in his cabin, about some few hundred square feet,
Sipping bowls of hot corn soup
under this shed was him and his tailors tiny troup.

Every button was stitched with finesse,
every lace found its place with ease.
The measuring tape in his hands he held
his customers with pride in him swelled.

15. Dripping Mozzarella cheese

Fragments of sole curry,
with snippets of Ginger
a dash of hot, black peppers
with a garnish of spluttering, yellow mustard.
Rosemary thyme
a glass of red wine,
dropped over stewed chicken,
dashes of burnt ,buttered onion crisps
with creamy, foamy, lather nicely whisked.
Rasberry umbrella crowing his glory,
sitting next to his dainty friend, Flaury.
Her umber, tanned skintone,
upon which her pink dress has she worn.
Those magenta shoe strings
resembling those glittery, neon rings,
his classy, v shaped cheekbones
looking like a man with a class of his own,
together they make merry
its even rumored, they may marry.

Sitting across the table as they nibble,
her glossy, red lips ,up and down, they almost dribble
sharing pleasantries, exchanging loving glances,
she may just say yes, I think there may be chances.
Holding that Velvet, red rose as his fingers advance,
a man quite handsome and bold, oh Holy, he's from
France.

This date is so princely
and it may even be costly,
a youthful, fair boy serenades,
under the shimmery moonlight that now radiates.
Is this love?,
It must be love,
'oh my darling', he whispers politely,
such adoration, she wont take lightly,
bouncing - leaping her heart beat swings,
like a fluttering firefly with dreamy, attractive wings.

Melting drops of white Mozzarella cheese,
upon chunky, cooked cubes of red meat,
roasted in hot, rising, glittery flames
lust upon love, does anybody blame?.
But no, that no longer is my game.

16. A fisher woman

Looking like a delicate damsel, but a strong woman,
a mother of four without any whim.
Unapologetic and Earthy
is this dark skinned, Sirathi.
Look at her big, luscious eyes,
those bow like lips ,
and quivering, large hips.
Her moon shaped nose ring
reflecting the light, as she joyfully sings,
with gay abandon ,
uttering lyrics at random.

Biju, Prabhas, Radha and Gopi
her children, rinsing their hands, still so soapy.
Her peppered hair strands ,
knotted with a fluorescent pink rubber band,
cleaning her latest catch, with her translucently veined
hands.
Her fingers are slender,
and sometimes we wonder

her zeal to go on,
of grit was she born.

'Gods own country', they call it,
living there since years, she hasn't moved even a bit.
Why did she catch my fancy,
it could even have been any Nancy,
was it her smile
that I noticed from a mile,
that rusticness perhaps,
and for some reason my heart claps.

She begins to comb those hair,
of Radha, her daughter, so fair,
pleating and dressing them in layers.
Biju, a boy of ten
finishing some school work, hes writing with his Blue
pen.
Prabhas, is younger
hanging some clothes on a broken hanger,
while Gopi is crying,
for her mother's attention is she vying.

A drunk old ma, lies closely on his charpoy
while narrating confabulated short tales of himself as a
young boy.
Sirathi's husband, now doing no job,

for him her heart still lovingly throbs.
A handyman once,
but now hes got this hunch
walking now with a slight stoop,
towards his hen, kept in a coop.

Amidst those tranquil backwaters,
is their modest little quarter,
surrounded by precious, green palms
at a distance are various old farms.
Merging with such cultural tapestry,
is their hairy dog, resembling somewhat a Husky,
a village, Indie dog
his ears rising up, listening to nearby croaking frogs.

Life of such a woman, a mystery in itself,
weaving threads of hardship, yet, joyful is her self.
Her eyes, still twinkling with a hopeful gleam,
in God she has faith to fulfill all her dreams.

17. Pigeons

Sitting by the fence,
a pretty flock so dense,
their soft, supple wings
fluttering and flapping, its Spring.

In that open park,
where sing many a Lark,
nestled together,
sitting by closely is a red- crested woodpecker.
And a Rosy mist, tints my window,
am watching them sitting on my sofa, indoors.

A halo forms
as the weather transforms,
Its getting dusky,
its kind of smelling musky.
Their stacatto feet, pitting and patting
the grounds softly, as they continue walking.

The night may be awakening

as their slim necks they are shaking,
hoping and gliding,
they appear to be sliding.
And one pigeon appears to be gazing,
his bands of Green and Blue shimmering,
Looking up at the starlight sky,
what could they be talking about and why?.

Some of them are trying to hide,
if they would in me confide
'Oh, tell me whats in your heart and mind,
am assuring you, I would be kind.

Tell me your lover's name,
let there be no reserve nor shame,
c'mon lets not make excuses, thats now so lame,
and you don't have to act even slightly tamed.

Brushing past the door,
oh why don't you fly indoor,
let us be friends,
talking about the latest trends.
If you could speak or perhaps you do,
why don't you join me in eating some hot Lentil stew.

And they are flying past
dropping off their casts,

time does have wings,
Its just one of those things.

Their sparkling bodies...taking a turn
getting ready are they now for their next run.

18. Let me be

I am too colorful for comfort,
you cant put me in a shell, no, am not a nerd.
Asking me to paint a series,
telling me they shouldn't really vary,
I prefer the play of drama,
as I paint wearing my multicolored pyjamas.

Not calling myself one bit conservative,
my art cannot be restrictive.
They may prefer kind of monotony,
this is quite a dichotomy,
let it flow, dribble and dazzle
in my bright gown, I may bedazzle.
Am not being modest, and I know
but about this let their be no row.

I fly above, in the blue skies so high,
its not even worth any try.
you say, tales or myths I must tell,
how will my love for art then swell?.

Leave me to my shores and let me be,
this is my request and a heartfelt plea.

Selling my art, may somewhere be a wish,
but for that, I ain't making no twist.
Desirous of boosting my image as an artist,
let it be natural, am enjoying the harvest.
Am not pretentious nor can I be
making reels, oh no,
like preventing honey from getting manufactured by a
bee .

19. The dragon boat race

The Reds are peering through the streets,
taking some respite from the Summer's heat.
With multicolored braids
as children and all folks raid
stalls selling ' Zongi', thats fondly home made.

A ceremonious time,
folks are relishing Realgar wine,
smearing children's faces,
avoiding any future harsh cases.
A Dragon shaped boat, dressed in natural wood
commemorating Qu Yuan, a long time, its stood.
As fellow Chinese men race,
keeping good pace,
following traditions,
its time for vacations.

Scattering rice into the waters,
around which many a fish may potter,
eating those grains,

preventing late Qu Yuan from any pain.

Those silken thread ribbons flying in the skies,
braided are children's hair, keeping away any cries.
With sticky rice dumplings are filled their plates,
suiting their culture, its perfect for their tastes.

Operas and songs may be sung across regions,
celebrating it all, certainly for valid reasons.
Bathing in floral, scented waters
before it gets any hotter,
wearing Vanilla perfume pouches,
while granny's may sit on their old couches.
Making an egg stand on its end,
without even an inch of bend
is considered good luck,
a ritual that has since then stuck.

Look at those festoons, those glaring red flags,
decorating those long boats, no there ain't any tags.
A carved Dragon head at the bow, it's tail at the rear
racing are they and to the end, they are near.
Colourful scales painted on the sides,
boats holding up fame, have reasons for their pride.

Bold, unabashed reds, pacing fast on a clear Blue palette,
glistening, under mighty rays are they strikingly lit.

Who will win is the mystery,
a game of frolic, involving a rich history.

Cultures are vast,
watching them, are children growing fast,
observing, learning
are the youth lovingly embibing.

My Chinese fantasy, finally put on paper,
telling stories, varied from those of sky scrapers.
Of reds and yellows did I want to write,
playing with words, as a poet, it's in my rights.

20. What poetry means to me

Fillers of love and joy,
are such words and phrases - a hoy!.
Moving away from the feeling of emptiness,
lock - stock and barrel to completeness.
Enhancing my life, this is such a gift
I wouldn't know the reasons for this shift.
Bowing and revering is now my trait,
seeking from this am I never a rebate.
No, its not a flimsy activity nor some time pass,
it's like a gardener, watering his vibrant, green grass.
Each word I scribble,
a blade of grass that dribbles,
adding adjectives and finding rhymes,
manuring and fertilising the soil each time.

A speck of molten Green,
a string of words with that glossy sheen.
Sparkly dew drops, in the morn appear
adding twists and turns, to some verses, I prepare.

That glistening Sunlight, every morning does bless,
with honey and sugar, these words I dress.

Loosing, immersing following the flow
writing new words and phrases in every row,
how blissful a treat is this from above,
nourishing and feeding my need for more love.

My pen holding my hand,
as in my palms, it merrily stands
sometimes slanting, enraptured in telling tales,
while breathing the freshness of ink, my heart inhales.

Oh, this must be a hobby or a source of recreation
reviving my sensibilities, a gift of true creation
honoring each work, with respect and regard,
next, i may be writing about some tribe and it's bard.

21. Don't miss this opportunity

How can you be so immersed in yourself,
today's a special day, its not just about ourselves.
Every day may be celebrated
but you don't have to get that calibrated,
no reasons do we ever need
for the Lord, irrespective of any caste or creed.

Time flies by, it may be eternal
Its nature is fraternal,
but don't take chances
and we must make advances
to revere and pray,
lifes not just how much you earn or pay.
And within minutes or even seconds
death may approach,
its not age bound, this thought you must re approach.
Dont wait for the last drop,
of river waters to harvest your crop,
don't drift and ponder,

life is a miraculous wonder.
An opportunity, you mustn't squash,
let not the end squeeze you, oh gosh.

His utterance is enough
and no its just not tough,
make it a way of life
behind trivias don't go and hide.

Its not about any fear,
oh, no my friend, sometimes dear,
but grab this opportunity
and live in that unity,
with love and compassion
without those so called comparisons.
It doesn't really matter what the crowds may think,
bathe in His love, before the eyes may finally close in a
blink.

Dont miss this opportunity,
even whilst being in your community,
pray and chant
or atleast once grant
yourself this favor,
His blessings we may savor.